CHOCOLATE COOKING

Edited by
Judy Ridgway

GALLERY BOOKS
An Imprint of W. H. Smith Publishers Inc.
112 Madison Avenue
New York City 10016

Contents

First published in hardcover in 1978
by Octopus Books Limited
59 Grosvenor Street, London W1

This edition published 1984 by Gallery Books
An imprint of W.H. Smith Publishers Inc.
112 Madison Avenue, New York, N.Y. 10016

© 1978 Octopus Books Limited

ISBN 0 8317 1290 2

Produced by Mandarin Publishers Limited
22a Westlands Road
Quarry Bay, Hong Kong

Printed in Hong Kong

Frontispiece: CHOCOLATE CHEESECAKE *(page 47),*
CHOCOLATE SOUFFLÉ *(page 43),*
PARTY FANCY CAKES *(page 11)*
(Photograph: Corning Limited – manufacturers of Pyrex)

INTRODUCTION

Chocolate must be one of the most popular flavourings in cooking today. Especially loved by children, this versatile ingredient can be used in many types of hot and cold desserts, cakes, cookies and confectionery.

Here you will find tempting chocolate gâteaux, cakes and cookies for family teas and special celebrations. A delicious selection of desserts covers every occasion – including family meals, dinner parties, and, of course, children's parties. The simply prepared attractive confectionery make ideal gifts at Christmas.

The Origin of Chocolate

Chocolate is produced from the cocoa bean, which grows in pods on cocoa trees. These originated in the Amazon forests of South America. The local Aztecs treated the cocoa bean with great respect using it to make a bitter drink, called 'chocolatl', a great delicacy at festivities.

The Spaniards were responsible for introducing this chocolate drink to Europe in the 17th century, but it remained an expensive luxury for many years. It was not until the beginning of the 19th century that chocolate was produced in a solid form for eating.

Nowadays, the chocolate produced in this country comes from cocoa beans grown in West Africa as well as South America. It takes an entire year's crop from one cocoa tree to produce about 500 g/1 lb of refined cocoa powder. This partly explains why cocoa is quite expensive.

The manufacture of cocoa powder entails a lengthy refining process. The cocoa beans are roasted, ground and sieved, and a large proportion of the cocoa butter is extracted, to produce the strongly-flavoured cocoa powder used extensively in cooking and drinks.

The processes for making eating chocolate are slightly different. Extra cocoa butter and sugar are added to refined cocoa to give dark (semi-sweet) chocolate. For milk chocolate, fresh milk is added at the same time. The ingredients are pummelled together until smooth.

Cooking with cocoa and chocolate

Cocoa is the most economical chocolate flavour for cooking, but it must be evenly blended into the mixture. It should either be sifted with other dry ingredients, or blended with a little boiling water to form a smooth paste before adding to the recipe.

Chocolate is normally melted before it is combined with other ingredients. Plain (semi-sweet) eating chocolate provides the best flavour. Less expensive 'cooking chocolate' and chocolate-flavoured chips are also obtainable. These have a cocoa base to which vegetable fats are added; technically they are not 'real' chocolate. Generally these products are easier to use in cooking for they melt more easily than eating chocolate but their flavour is inferior.

Melting chocolate: Chocolate should be broken into pieces, then melted in a double boiler, or a heatproof bowl over a small pan of hot, not boiling, water. The water must be kept below simmering to prevent steam from coming into contact with the chocolate. If this happens, or if water is added to the chocolate, or the chocolate is overheated, it will immediately solidify to form a stiff mass. Sometimes this can be rectified by adding 1 or 2 tablespoons of vegetable shortening, but it is best avoided.

Chocolate Decorations:

Chocolate can be melted and used to prepare a variety of attractive and easy to make decorations, such as triangles, rounds, curls and leaves, for adding a professional finish to gâteaux and desserts.

Making chocolate shapes: Draw out your chosen designs, e.g. holly leaves, on a piece of paper and place under a sheet of greaseproof (wax) paper. Place the melted chocolate in a paper piping bag without a nozzle and, just before starting to pipe, snip off a small piece from the point of the bag. The chocolate will run freely with a little pressure. Carefully pipe onto the greaseproof (wax) paper following the outline of the shapes. Fill the centres as necessary. Leave until hardened then carefully remove from the paper.

Alternatively spread the melted chocolate onto a piece of greaseproof (wax) paper and smooth flat with a palette knife. Leave until set but not hard, and cut out shapes, using pastry cutters, or a sharp knife. Allow to harden completely before removing from the paper.

Chocolate rose leaves: Wash and dry the leaves. Using a fine paint brush, coat the underside of each leaf with melted chocolate. Place the leaves on a plate and chill in the refrigerator until set. When hard, peel the leaf away from the chocolate and use as required.

Making chocolate caraque: It is important to use good quality plain (semi-sweet) chocolate for making caraque. Spread a thin layer of melted chocolate onto a marble or formica surface using a palette knife. Leave until set but not hard. Hold a sharp knife at a 45° angle to the chocolate to shave off long curls. Move carefully as these curls are fragile and break easily.

Making small chocolate curls: It is possible to make curls with a vegetable peeler on some softer varieties of chocolate without having to melt it. Using a vegetable peeler, scrape along the surface of a block of chocolate to shave off curls.

MAKING CHOCOLATE DECORATIONS
(Photograph: Cadbury Typhoo Food Advisory Service)

SMALL CAKES AND COOKIES

Coconut Slices

METRIC/IMPERIAL	AMERICAN
100 g/4 oz unsalted butter	½ cup sweet butter
175 g/6 oz caster sugar	¾ cup sugar
2 eggs	2 eggs
100 g/4 oz ground rice	⅔ cup ground rice
100 g/4 oz desiccated coconut	1⅓ cups shredded coconut
100 g/4 oz sultanas	⅔ cup seedless white raisins
100 g/4 oz glacé cherries, chopped	½ cup chopped candied cherries
175 g/6 oz plain chocolate	1 cup semi-sweet chocolate chips

Cream the butter and sugar together until soft. Gradually beat in the eggs. Fold in the rice, coconut, sultanas (raisins) and cherries. Spoon the mixture into a lined and greased 28 × 18 cm/11 × 7 inch shallow cake tin (pan) and spread evenly. Cook in a moderate oven (160°C/325°F, Gas Mark 3) for 30 minutes. Leave to cool in the tin (pan).

   Melt the chocolate in a bowl over hot water, then pour over the biscuit (cookie) base. Leave until set, then cut into bars and remove from the tin (pan).
Makes 12

Party Fancy Cakes

METRIC/IMPERIAL	AMERICAN
75 g/3 oz cocoa powder	¾ cup unsweetened cocoa
2 tablespoons hot water	2 tablespoons hot water
350 g/12 oz butter	1½ cups butter
350 g/12 oz caster sugar	1½ cups sugar
6 eggs	6 eggs
350 g/12 oz self-raising flour, sifted	3 cups sifted self-rising flour
Glacé icings:	**Glacé icings:**
450 g/1 lb icing sugar, sifted	3½ cups sifted confectioners' sugar
120 ml/4 fl oz water	½ cup water
2 teaspoons cocoa powder mixed with 1 teaspoon hot water	2 teaspoons unsweetened cocoa mixed with 1 teaspoon hot water
1 tablespoon coffee essence	1 tablespoon coffee extract
To decorate:	**To decorate:**
Chocolate buttercream	Chocolate butter cream
Coffee buttercream	Coffee butter cream
plain chocolate, melted	semi-sweet chocolate, melted
chocolate caraque	chocolate caraque
chocolate squares and triangles	chocolate squares and triangles

Blend the cocoa with the hot water and set aside. Cream the butter and sugar together in a bowl until light and fluffy. Beat in the eggs, one at a time, adding a tablespoon of the flour with each one. Fold in the remaining flour with the cocoa mixture.

Spoon into a greased and lined 23 × 35 cm/9 × 14 inch baking tin (pan) or ovenproof dish. Bake in a moderate oven (180°C/350°F, Gas Mark 4) for 40 to 45 minutes or until firm to the touch. Turn out onto a wire rack to cool. Cut into 5 × 5.5 cm/2 × 2¼ inch squares and replace on the wire rack.

To make the glacé icings, mix the icing (confectioners') sugar with the water, and beat to a smooth paste. Halve the mixture and flavour one portion with the blended cocoa and the other with the coffee essence (extract). Coat each cake completely with one of the glacé icings. Leave until set.

Prepare the chocolate buttercream as for Mocha Slice (see page 40) and the coffee buttercream as for Chocolate Banana Cake (see page 31). Decorate the cakes with piped buttercream and piped melted chocolate (as illustrated on page 4), finishing with chocolate caraque, squares and triangles (see page 8).
Makes 28 cakes

Chocolate Crackles

METRIC/IMPERIAL	AMERICAN
100 g/4 oz plain chocolate	2/3 cup semi-sweet chocolate chips
100 g/4 oz butter	1/2 cup butter
4 tablespoons golden syrup	4 tablespoons light corn syrup
100 g/4 oz cornflakes	4 cups cornflakes
175 g/6 oz dates, stoned and	1 cup pitted dates, chopped
chopped	1/2 cup chopped walnuts
50 g/2 oz walnuts, chopped	

Melt the chocolate in a bowl over hot water. Place the butter and syrup in a small pan over gentle heat and stir until the butter is melted. Stir into the chocolate with the remaining ingredients and mix well.

Allow to cool slightly, then place heaped spoonfuls of the mixture into paper cases (bonbon cups) and leave until firm.
Makes 18 to 20

Chocolate Flapjacks

METRIC/IMPERIAL	AMERICAN
75 g/3 oz butter	6 tablespoons butter
2 tablespoons golden syrup	2 tablespoons light corn syrup
225 g/8 oz Muesli mix	1/2 lb Muesli mix
100 g/4 oz stoned dates, chopped	1/2 cup chopped pitted dates
50 g/2 oz glacé cherries, chopped	1/4 cup candied cherries, chopped
100 g/4 oz plain chocolate	2/3 cup semi-sweet chocolate chips

Heat the butter and syrup together in a saucepan until melted. Remove from the heat and add the Muesli mix, dates and cherries. Mix thoroughly. Spoon into a greased 18 cm/7 inch square cake tin (pan) and press down well. Chill until firm, then remove from the tin (pan).

Melt the chocolate in a bowl over hot water. Spread over the flapjack mixture and mark into swirls with a palette knife. Chill until the chocolate is firm. Cut into fingers before serving.
Makes 10

KRISPIE FLORENTINES *(page 14)*, CHOCOLATE CRACKLES,
CHOCOLATE FLAPJACKS
(Photograph: Kelloggs Limited)

Krispie Florentines

METRIC/IMPERIAL
50 g/2 oz butter
1 tablespoon honey
50 g/2 oz stoned dates, chopped
50 g/2 oz seedless raisins
50 g/2 oz glacé cherries, chopped
1 tablespoon chopped almonds
1 tablespoon chopped walnuts
50 g/2 oz Rice Krispies
Topping:
175 g/6 oz plain chocolate
2 tablespoons milk

AMERICAN
¼ cup butter
1 tablespoon honey
¼ cup chopped pitted dates
⅓ cup seedless raisins
¼ cup candied cherries, chopped
1 tablespoon chopped almonds
1 tablespoon chopped walnuts
2 cups Rice Krispies
Topping:
1 cup semi-sweet chocolate chips
2 tablespoons milk

Place the butter and honey in a saucepan and heat gently until the butter is melted. Add the dates and cook for 1 minute, stirring constantly. Remove from the heat and stir in the raisins, cherries, nuts and Rice Krispies. Mix thoroughly. Turn into a greased 18 cm/7 inch square shallow tin (pan) and press down firmly.

To make the topping, melt the chocolate with the milk in a bowl over hot water, stirring frequently. Pour over the florentine base and spread evenly. Chill until set, then cut into squares or fingers.
Makes 12

Chocolate Butter Kisses

METRIC/IMPERIAL
75 g/3 oz unsalted butter
75 g/3 oz caster sugar
100 g/4 oz plain flour
2 tablespoons cocoa powder
1 teaspoon baking powder
pinch of salt
100 g/4 oz seedless raisins, chopped
25 g/1 oz walnuts, chopped
1 tablespoon milk
Filling:
25 g/1 oz unsalted butter
1 tablespoon milk
100 g/4 oz icing sugar
2 tablespoons cocoa powder
To decorate:
sifted icing sugar

AMERICAN
1/3 cup sweet butter
3/4 cup sugar
1 cup all-purpose flour
2 tablespoons unsweetened cocoa
1 teaspoon baking powder
pinch of salt
3/4 cup seedless raisins, chopped
1/4 cup chopped walnuts
1 tablespoon milk
Filling:
2 tablespoons sweet butter
1 tablespoon milk
1 cup confectioners' sugar
2 tablespoons unsweetened cocoa
To decorate:
sifted confectioners' sugar

Cream the butter and sugar until light and fluffy. Sift the flour, cocoa, baking powder and salt together and work into the butter mixture. Add the raisins, nuts and milk and mix thoroughly.

Place teaspoonfuls of the mixture, well apart, on greased baking sheets. Bake in a moderately hot oven (190°C/375°F, Gas Mark 5) for 20 minutes. Leave for 2 minutes, then carefully transfer to a wire rack to cool completely.

To make the filling, heat the butter and milk in a small pan until melted. Sift the icing (confectioners') sugar and cocoa together into a bowl. Gradually add the butter and milk mixture and beat thoroughly until well mixed.

Sandwich the biscuits (cookies) together in pairs with the filling and sprinkle with icing (confectioners') sugar.
Makes 12

Caramel Fingers

METRIC/IMPERIAL	AMERICAN
100 g/4 oz unsalted butter	*½ cup sweet butter*
50 g/2 oz caster sugar	*¼ cup sugar*
175 g/6 oz plain flour, sifted	*1½ cups all-purpose flour, sifted*
Topping:	**Topping:**
1 small can condensed milk	*1 small can condensed milk*
100 g/4 oz caster sugar	*½ cup sugar*
100 g/4 oz unsalted butter	*½ cup sweet butter*
2 tablespoons golden syrup	*2 tablespoons light corn syrup*
175 g/6 oz plain chocolate	*1 cup semi-sweet chocolate chips*

Cream the butter and sugar together until light and fluffy. Add the flour and stir until the mixture binds together. Knead until smooth. Press the mixture into the base of a greased shallow 20 cm/8 inch square tin (pan). Prick all over and bake in a moderate oven (180°C/350°F, Gas Mark 4) for 20 to 30 minutes until golden brown. Leave to cool slightly, then remove from the tin (pan) and place on a wire rack.

For the topping, place the condensed milk, sugar, butter and golden (light corn) syrup in a pan and heat gently until the sugar is dissolved, then boil for 6 to 8 minutes, stirring all the time. Remove from the heat and allow to cool slightly.

Pour the caramel topping over the biscuit (cookie) base and allow to cool thoroughly. Melt the chocolate in a bowl over hot water and spread over the caramel. Mark into portions and leave to set. Serve cut into fingers.

Makes 24

CHOCOLATE ÉCLAIRS *(page 18)*,
CHOCOLATE BUTTER KISSES *(page 15)*, CARAMEL FINGERS
(Photograph: Wheelbarrow Unsalted Dutch Butter)

Chocolate Éclairs

METRIC/IMPERIAL
50 g/2 oz unsalted butter
150 ml/¼ pint water
65 g/2½ oz plain flour, sifted
2 eggs, beaten
Filling:
300 ml/½ pint double cream,
  whipped
Topping:
100 g/4 oz plain chocolate
25 g/1 oz unsalted butter

AMERICAN
¼ cup sweet butter
⅔ cup water
⅔ cup all-purpose flour, sifted
2 eggs, beaten
Filling:
1¼ cups heavy cream, whipped
Topping:
⅔ cup semi-sweet chocolate chips
2 tablespoons sweet butter

Melt the butter in a saucepan over low heat. Add the water and bring to the boil. Remove from the heat and add the flour. Beat well with a wooden spoon until the mixture leaves the sides of the pan clean. Add the eggs, a little at a time, beating well between each addition; the choux paste should be shiny and thick enough to hold its shape.

Spoon the mixture into a piping bag fitted with a 1 cm/½ inch nozzle and pipe 7.5 cm/3 inch lengths onto a lightly greased baking sheet. Bake in a hot oven (220°C/425°F, Gas Mark 7) for 20 to 25 minutes until crisp and golden brown. Make a slit in the side of each éclair to allow the steam to escape and transfer to a wire rack to cool.

Just before serving, fill the éclairs with the whipped cream. Melt the chocolate and butter in a bowl over hot water. Cool until beginning to thicken, then dip the top of each éclair into the chocolate. Leave to set.
Makes 12

Chocolate Cream Buns

Prepare the mixture as above. Place heaped tablespoonfuls on a lightly greased baking sheet, spacing well apart. Bake in the centre of a moderately hot oven (200°C/400°F, Gas Mark 6) for 40 to 45 minutes until golden brown and cooked through. Split, cool on a wire rack, then fill with whipped cream and top with chocolate as above.

Note: Using an electric blender or cream maker you can make your own cream as follows: Place 120 ml/4 fl oz (½ cup) milk in a pan and add 100 g/4 oz (½ cup) unsalted (sweet) butter, cut into small pieces. Heat gently until the butter is melted, then transfer to a blender or cream maker. Blend the mixture or pump through the cream maker. Stir and chill in the refrigerator for 2 to 3 hours. Whisk until stiff.

Melting Moments

METRIC/IMPERIAL
100 g/4 oz butter, softened
50 g/2 oz icing sugar, sifted
2 teaspoons lemon juice
75 g/3 oz plain flour, sifted
75 g/3 oz self-raising flour, sifted
Filling:
25 g/1 oz butter, softened
75 g/3 oz icing sugar, sifted
1 teaspoon lemon juice
To finish:
50 g/2 oz plain chocolate

AMERICAN
½ cup butter, softened
½ cup confectioners' sugar, sifted
2 teaspoons lemon juice
¾ cup all-purpose flour, sifted
¾ cup self-rising flour, sifted
Filling:
2 tablespoons softened butter
¾ cup confectioners' sugar, sifted
1 teaspoon lemon juice
To finish:
⅓ cup semi-sweet chocolate chips

Beat the butter and sugar together until light and fluffy. Stir in the lemon juice and flours. Mix to a fairly stiff dough.

Place the mixture in a piping bag fitted with a 1 cm/½ inch fluted nozzle and pipe 6 cm/2½ inch lengths onto greased baking sheets, spacing well apart. Bake in a moderately hot oven (190°C/375°F, Gas Mark 5) for 10 to 15 minutes until golden brown. Cool on a wire rack.

For the filling, beat the butter and sugar together until light and fluffy and stir in the lemon juice. Sandwich the biscuits (cookies) together in pairs with the filling. Melt the chocolate in a bowl over hot water, and dip both ends of the biscuits (cookies) into the chocolate. Leave on a wire rack until the chocolate is firm.
Makes 12

Siena Cake

METRIC/IMPERIAL
75 g/3 oz hazelnuts, toasted,
  skinned and chopped
75 g/3 oz blanched almonds,
  coarsely chopped
175 g/6 oz candied peel, finely
  chopped
25 g/1 oz cocoa powder
50 g/2 oz plain flour
½ teaspoon ground cinnamon
¼ teaspoon ground mixed spice
100 g/4 oz caster sugar
100 g/4 oz clear honey
Topping:
2 tablespoons icing sugar
1 teaspoon ground cinnamon

AMERICAN
⅔ cup filberts, toasted, skinned and
  chopped
¾ cup coarsely chopped blanched
  almonds
1 cup finely chopped candied peel
¼ cup unsweetened cocoa
½ cup all-purpose flour
½ teaspoon ground cinnamon
¼ teaspoon ground nutmeg
½ cup sugar
⅓ cup clear honey
Topping:
2 tablespoons confectioners' sugar
1 teaspoon ground cinnamon

Mix together the hazelnuts (filberts), almonds, candied peel, cocoa, flour and spices.

Put the sugar and honey into a small pan, heat gently until the sugar dissolves, then boil steadily until a sugar thermometer registers 115°C/240°F or until a little of the mixture dropped into a cup of cold water forms a soft ball. Take off the heat immediately and stir in the nut mixture.

Turn into a lined and greased 20 cm/8 inch flan ring (pie pan), spread evenly and press down firmly. Bake in a cool oven (150°C/300°F, Gas Mark 2) for 30 to 35 minutes.

Allow to cool then turn out and sprinkle the top liberally with the icing (confectioners') sugar, sifted with the cinnamon. Cut into small wedges before serving.
Makes 8 to 12

Jam Jewels

METRIC/IMPERIAL	AMERICAN
100 g/4 oz margarine	½ cup margarine
75 g/3 oz caster sugar	6 tablespoons sugar
2 eggs	2 eggs
100 g/4 oz self-raising flour, sifted	1 cup self-rising flour, sifted
25 g/1 oz cocoa	¼ cup unsweetened cocoa
1 tablespoon hot water	1 tablespoon hot water
Icing:	**Frosting:**
250 g/9 oz icing sugar, sifted	2 cups confectioners' sugar, sifted
100 g/4 oz butter	½ cup butter
1 tablespoon milk	1 tablespoon milk
25 g/1 oz cocoa powder	¼ cup unsweetened cocoa
1 tablespoon hot water	1 tablespoon hot water
To decorate:	**To decorate:**
50 g/2 oz plain chocolate, grated	2 squares semi-sweet chocolate, grated
50 g/2 oz raspberry jam	3 tablespoons raspberry jelly
50 g/2 oz apricot jam	3 tablespoons apricot jelly

Cream the margarine and sugar together until fluffy. Beat in the eggs with a little flour. When smooth fold in the remaining flour and cocoa mixed with water. Spread into a lined and greased 18 × 28 cm/ 7 × 11 inch shallow cake tin (pan), hollowing out the centre a little. Bake in a moderately hot oven (190°C/375°F, Gas Mark 5) for about 25 minutes until well risen. Turn out onto a wire rack to cool.

Beat the icing (confectioners') sugar and butter with the milk until smooth. Put three quarters of the mixture into a piping bag fitted with a star (fluted) nozzle. Mix the cocoa with the water and beat into the remaining icing (frosting).

Cut the cake into 15 even sized squares. Spread the chocolate icing (frosting) around the sides then press on the grated chocolate. Pipe small rosettes around the edge of the top of each cake. Fill the centres with the jams (jellies).
Makes 15

Honey Cookies

METRIC/IMPERIAL
50 g/2 oz plain flour
50 g/2 oz custard powder
50 g/2 oz butter
*50 g/2 oz plain chocolate, finely
  chopped*
1 tablespoon clear honey
1 egg yolk

AMERICAN
½ cup all-purpose flour
*½ cup Bird's English Imported
  Dessert Mix*
¼ cup butter
⅓ cup semi-sweet chocolate chips
1 tablespoon clear honey
1 egg yolk

Sift the flour and custard powder (dessert mix) together into a bowl. Rub in the butter until the mixture resembles fine breadcrumbs. Add the chocolate and stir well. Blend the honey with the egg yolk and add to the dry ingredients. Mix to a smooth dough.

Knead lightly, then roll out the dough on a floured board to a 1 cm/½ inch thickness. Cut into 5 cm/2 inch rounds, using a plain cutter. Place on a greased baking sheet and bake in a cool oven (150°C/300°F, Gas Mark 2) for 25 to 30 minutes. Cool on a wire rack.
Makes 15

Chocolate Chip Cookies

METRIC/IMPERIAL
225 g/8 oz plain flour
1 teaspoon baking powder
100 g/4 oz unsalted butter
*75 g/3 oz plain chocolate, finely
  chopped*
175 g/6 oz caster sugar
1 egg, beaten
1 teaspoon vanilla essence

AMERICAN
2 cups all-purpose flour
1 teaspoon baking powder
½ cup sweet butter
½ cup semi-sweet chocolate chips
¾ cup sugar
1 egg, beaten
1 teaspoon vanilla extract

Sift the flour and baking powder into a bowl. Rub in the butter until the mixture resembles fine breadcrumbs. Stir in the chocolate and sugar. Add the egg and vanilla essence (extract) and mix to a stiff dough.

Transfer the dough to a floured board and shape into a roll, about 45 cm/18 inches long. Wrap in foil and chill in the refrigerator for 1 hour.

Remove the foil and cut the roll into approximately 40 slices. Place, well apart, on greased baking sheets. Bake in a moderately hot oven (190°C/375°F, Gas Mark 5) for 10 to 12 minutes. Cool on a wire rack.
Makes 40

Chocolate Walnut Cookies

METRIC/IMPERIAL	AMERICAN
100 g/4 oz butter	*½ cup butter*
50 g/2 oz caster sugar	*¼ cup sugar*
175 g/6 oz self-raising flour, sifted	*1½ cups self-rising flour, sifted*
2 tablespoons condensed milk	*2 tablespoons condensed milk*
25 g/1 oz walnuts, finely chopped	*¼ cup finely chopped walnuts*
100 g/4 oz plain chocolate, grated	*4 squares semi-sweet chocolate, grated*

Beat the butter and sugar together until light and fluffy. Work in half the flour, then stir in the condensed milk. Add the remaining flour, walnuts and chocolate. Mix thoroughly.

Roll teaspoonfuls of the mixture into balls. Place on greased baking sheets and flatten slightly. Bake in a moderate oven (180°C/350°F, Gas Mark 4) for about 15 minutes. Cool on a wire rack.
Makes 25

Dutch Cream Delights

METRIC/IMPERIAL	AMERICAN
100 g/4 oz butter, softened	*½ cup butter, softened*
50 g/2 oz caster sugar	*¼ cup sugar*
100 g/4 oz plain flour	*1 cup all-purpose flour*
25 g/1 oz cornflour	*¼ cup cornstarch*
2 tablespoons cocoa powder	*2 tablespoons unsweetened cocoa*
25 g/1 oz almonds, chopped	*¼ cup chopped almonds*
Filling:	**Filling:**
300 ml/½ pint double cream, whipped	*1¼ cups heavy cream, whipped*
175 g/6 oz strawberries, halved	*1¼ cups strawberries, halved*
To decorate:	**To decorate:**
sifted icing sugar	*sifted confectioners' sugar*

Cream together the butter and sugar until light and fluffy. Sift the flour, cornflour (cornstarch) and cocoa together and gradually beat into the mixture. Stir in the almonds.

Knead the dough lightly, then roll out to a 5 mm/¼ inch thickness and cut into 12 squares using a 6 cm/2½ inch fluted cutter. Transfer to greased baking sheets and bake in a moderate oven (180°C/350°F, Gas Mark 4) for 15 to 20 minutes until lightly browned. Cool on a wire rack.

Pipe the cream onto half the squares. Top with the strawberries and remaining squares. Dust with icing (confectioners') sugar.
Makes 6

DUTCH CREAM DELIGHTS
(Photograph: Dutch Dairy Bureau)

LARGE CAKES AND GÂTEAUX

Chocolate Layer Cake

METRIC/IMPERIAL
25 g/1 oz cocoa powder
1 tablespoon hot water
100 g/4 oz butter
100 g/4 oz caster sugar
2 eggs, beaten
100 g/4 oz self-raising flour, sifted
Buttercream:
50 g/2 oz butter, softened
100 g/4 oz icing sugar, sifted
½ teaspoon vanilla essence
40 g/1½ oz plain chocolate, melted
1 tablespoon milk
To decorate:
icing sugar for dusting

AMERICAN
¼ cup unsweetened cocoa powder
1 tablespoon hot water
½ cup butter
½ cup sugar
2 eggs, beaten
1 cup self-rising flour, sifted
Buttercream:
¼ cup butter, softened
1 cup confectioners' sugar, sifted
½ teaspoon vanilla extract
1½ squares semi-sweet chocolate,
  melted
1 tablespoon milk
To decorate:
confectioners' sugar for dusting

Mix the cocoa and water together and leave to cool. Cream the butter and sugar together until light and fluffy. Beat in the eggs one at a time with a spoonful of flour. Fold in the remaining flour with the cooled cocoa mixture.

Spoon into two lined and greased 18 cm/7 inch sandwich tins (layer cake pans). Bake in a moderately hot oven (190°C/375°F, Gas Mark 5) for about 20 minutes or until well risen and firm to the touch. Turn onto a wire rack to cool.

To make the buttercream, beat the butter and sugar together until smooth. Add the vanilla essence (extract), chocolate and enough milk to make a smooth and firm spreading consistency.

Sandwich the cakes with the buttercream and dust the top with icing (confectioners') sugar.
Makes one 18 cm/7 inch cake

Nutty Orange Tea Bread

METRIC/IMPERIAL
350 g/12 oz self-raising flour
pinch of salt
75 g/3 oz caster sugar
50 g/2 oz walnuts or pecan nuts,
  chopped
50 g/2 oz candied peel, chopped
grated rind of 2 oranges
2 eggs
150 ml/¼ pint orange juice
2 tablespoons milk
50 g/2 oz butter, melted
50 g/2 oz plain chocolate, grated

AMERICAN
3 cups self-rising flour, sifted
pinch of salt
6 tablespoons sugar
½ cup chopped walnuts or pecan
  nuts
⅓ cup chopped candied peel
grated rind of 2 oranges
2 eggs
⅔ cup orange juice
2 tablespoons milk
¼ cup butter, melted
2 squares semi-sweet chocolate,
  grated

Sift the flour and salt into a bowl. Stir in the sugar, nuts, peel and orange rind. Beat the eggs with the orange juice and milk and pour over the dry ingredients. Mix thoroughly, gradually adding the melted butter. Grease and flour a 1 kg/2 lb loaf tin (pan) and spoon in one third of the mixture. Sprinkle with one third of the grated chocolate. Repeat these layers twice.

Bake in a moderate oven (160°C/325°F, Gas Mark 3) for about 1 hour or until a skewer inserted into the centre of the cake comes out clean. Remove from the tin (pan) and cool on a wire rack. Serve sliced with butter.

Makes one 1 kg/2 lb cake

Chocolate Orange Cake

METRIC/IMPERIAL
2 tablespoons cocoa powder
2 tablespoons hot water
100 g/4 oz butter
150 g/5 oz caster sugar
2 eggs, beaten
100 g/4 oz self-raising flour, sifted
grated rind of 1 orange
1 tablespoon orange juice
Chocolate icing:
50 g/2 oz plain chocolate
25 g/1 oz butter
25 g/1 oz icing sugar, sifted
To decorate:
few orange jelly slices

AMERICAN
2 tablespoons unsweetened cocoa
2 tablespoons hot water
½ cup butter
⅔ cup sugar
2 eggs, beaten
1 cup self-rising flour, sifted
grated rind of 1 orange
1 tablespoon orange juice
Chocolate frosting:
⅓ cup semi-sweet chocolate chips
2 tablespoons butter
¼ cup sifted confectioners' sugar
To decorate:
few orange candy slices

Blend the cocoa with the water and leave to cool. Cream the butter and sugar together until light and fluffy. Beat in the cocoa mixture. Beat in the eggs, with a little flour. Fold in the remaining flour, the orange rind and juice.

Turn into a lined and greased 18 cm/7 inch round cake tin (pan) and spread evenly. Bake in a moderate oven (180°C/350°F, Gas Mark 4) for 40 to 50 minutes or until firm to the touch. Turn onto a wire rack to cool.

To make the icing (frosting), melt the chocolate in a bowl over hot water, then beat in the butter. Remove from the heat and add the icing (confectioners') sugar. Beat until smooth. Quickly spread over the top of the cake and mark into swirls using a palette knife. Decorate with orange jelly (candy) slices.

Makes one 18 cm (7 inch) cake

Chocolate Ribbon Cake

METRIC/IMPERIAL
225 g/8 oz plain flour
pinch of salt
2 teaspoons baking powder
75 g/3 oz margarine
75 g/3 oz caster sugar
1 egg, beaten
½ teaspoon vanilla essence
150 ml/¼ pint milk
100 g/4 oz plain chocolate, coarsely
  grated
icing sugar to decorate

AMERICAN
2 cups all-purpose flour
pinch of salt
2 teaspoons baking powder
6 tablespoons margarine
6 tablespoons sugar
1 egg, beaten
½ teaspoon vanilla extract
⅔ cup milk
4 squares semi-sweet chocolate,
  coarsely grated
confectioners' sugar to decorate

Sift the flour, salt and baking powder into a mixing bowl. Rub the margarine into the flour until the mixture resembles fine breadcrumbs. Add the sugar, egg, vanilla essence (extract) and milk, and stir with a wooden spoon until smooth; the mixture should have a soft dropping consistency.

Spoon a third of the cake mixture into a lined and greased 15 cm/6 inch round cake tin (pan) and sprinkle a third of the chocolate over the top. Continue these layers, finishing with a layer of chocolate. Bake in a moderately hot oven (190°C/375°F, Gas Mark 5) for 15 minutes, then reduce the heat to (180°C/350°F, Gas Mark 4) and bake for a further 1 hour.

Turn out and place on a wire rack to cool. Sprinkle with icing (confectioners') sugar before serving.

Makes one 15 cm/6 inch cake

Chocolate Banana Cake

METRIC/IMPERIAL
175 g/6 oz unsalted butter
175 g/6 oz caster sugar
3 eggs
225 g/8 oz self-raising flour, sifted
2 ripe bananas, mashed
Chocolate buttercream:
25 g/1 oz cocoa powder
1 tablespoon hot water
75 g/3 oz butter
175 g/6 oz icing sugar, sifted
Glacé icing:
225 g/8 oz icing sugar, sifted
3-4 tablespoons water
2 teaspoons cocoa powder
1 teaspoon hot water
To decorate:
chocolate vermicelli

AMERICAN
3/4 cup sweet butter
3/4 cup sugar
3 eggs
2 cups self-rising flour, sifted
2 ripe bananas, mashed
Chocolate buttercream:
1/4 cup unsweetened cocoa
1 tablespoon hot water
1/3 cup butter
1 1/3 cups sifted confectioners' sugar
Glacé icing:
1 3/4 cups sifted confectioners' sugar
3-4 tablespoons water
2 teaspoons unsweetened cocoa
1 teaspoon hot water
To decorate:
chocolate sprinkles

Cream the butter and sugar together until light and fluffy. Beat in the eggs, one at a time, adding a little of the flour with each one. Fold in the remaining flour and the bananas.

Divide the mixture between two greased 20 cm/8 inch round sandwich tins (layer cake pans). Bake in a moderately hot oven (190°C/375°F, Gas Mark 5) for 25 to 30 minutes. Turn out onto a wire rack to cool.

To make the buttercream, blend the cocoa with the water and allow to cool. Cream the butter and sugar together until smooth, then beat in the cocoa mixture. Sandwich the two cakes together with half the buttercream and spread the remainder round the sides. Roll the sides in the chocolate vermicelli (sprinkles) to coat evenly.

To make the glacé icing, mix the icing (confectioners') sugar with the water, and beat to a smooth paste. Spread three quarters of the icing over the top of the cake. Blend the cocoa with the hot water and add to the remaining icing. Mix thoroughly. Place in a piping bag fitted with a small plain nozzle and pipe straight lines across the cake and then lines at right angles to form squares.

Makes one 20 cm/8 inch cake

Chequered Cake

METRIC/IMPERIAL
225 g/8 oz butter
225 g/8 oz caster sugar
4 eggs, beaten
225 g/8 oz plain flour
pinch of salt
2 teaspoons baking powder
25 g/1 oz cocoa powder
1 tablespoon hot water
Buttercream:
75 g/3 oz butter
225 g/8 oz icing sugar, sifted
1-2 tablespoons milk
50 g/2 oz plain chocolate, melted
To decorate:
chocolate curls made with 175 g/
  6 oz plain chocolate (see page 8)
sifted icing sugar

AMERICAN
1 cup butter
1 cup sugar
4 eggs, beaten
2 cups all-purpose flour
pinch of salt
2 teaspoons baking powder
¼ cup unsweetened cocoa
1 tablespoon hot water
Buttercream:
6 tablespoons butter
2 cups sifted confectioners' sugar
1-2 tablespoons milk
2 squares semi-sweet chocolate,
  melted
To decorate:
chocolate curls made with 6 squares
  semi-sweet chocolate (see page 8)
sifted confectioners' sugar

Cream the butter and sugar together until light and fluffy. Beat in the eggs, one at a time, adding a little flour with each one. Sift the remaining flour, salt and baking powder together and fold into the mixture. Divide the mixture in half. Mix the cocoa and water together and fold into one half of the mixture.

Divide the plain and chocolate mixtures between three greased and lined 15 cm/6 inch sandwich tins (cake layer pans), arranging the mixtures in alternate rows across. Bake in a moderate oven (180°C/350°F, Gas Mark 4) for about 25 to 30 minutes. Turn out of the tins (pans) and leave to cool on a wire rack.

Cream the butter and sugar together with a little milk. Beat well, then mix in the chocolate. Use half the buttercream to sandwich the cakes together, placing them at right angles to each other to give the cake a chequered effect when cut. Spread the rest of the buttercream over the top and sides of the cake.

Press small chocolate curls around the sides of the cake. Arrange the larger curls on the top in parallel lines and sprinkle icing (confectioners') sugar over the top to form a pattern.

Makes one 15 cm/6 inch cake

CHOCOLATE CHESTNUT GATEAU *(page 35)*, CHEQUERED CAKE, CHOCOLATE PEPPERMINT CAKE *(page 34)*
(Photograph: British Sugar Bureau)

Chocolate Peppermint Cake

METRIC/IMPERIAL

100 g/4 oz self-raising flour
50 g/2 oz cocoa powder
25 g/1 oz drinking chocolate
100 g/4 oz butter
100 g/4 oz sugar
2 eggs, beaten
75 g/3 oz ground almonds
1 tablespoon strong black coffee
1 tablespoon sherry
Buttercream:
50 g/2 oz butter
100 g/4 oz icing sugar, sifted
50 g/2 oz drinking chocolate
1 tablespoon water
few drops of peppermint essence
Icing:
100 g/4 oz plain chocolate
1 tablespoon sherry
50 g/2 oz butter
50 g/2 oz icing sugar, sifted
To decorate:
120 ml/4 fl oz double cream,
 whipped
4 square chocolate mint creams
8 glacé cherries

AMERICAN

1 cup self-rising flour
1/2 cup unsweetened cocoa
1/4 cup sweetened cocoa
1/2 cup butter
1/2 cup sugar
2 eggs, beaten
3/4 cup ground almonds
1 tablespoon strong black coffee
1 tablespoon sherry
Buttercream:
1/4 cup butter
1 cup confectioners' sugar, sifted
1/2 cup sweetened cocoa
1 tablespoon water
few drops of peppermint extract
Frosting:
2/3 cup semi-sweet chocolate chips
1 tablespoon sherry
2 tablespoons butter
1/2 cup confectioners' sugar, sifted
To decorate:
1/2 cup heavy cream, whipped
4 square chocolate mint creams
8 candied cherries

Sift the flour, cocoa and chocolate powder together. Cream the butter and sugar together until light and fluffy. Beat in the eggs, one at a time. Fold in the flour and almonds alternately with the coffee and sherry.

Spoon the mixture into a lined and greased 20 cm/8 inch deep round cake tin (pan). Bake in a moderate oven (180°C/350°F, Gas Mark 4) for about 45 minutes. Remove from the tin (pan) and cool on a wire rack.

To make the buttercream, beat the butter and icing (confectioners') sugar together. Add the drinking chocolate (sweetened cocoa), water and peppermint to taste. Beat until smooth. Slice the cake into two layers and sandwich together with the peppermint filling.

To make the icing (frosting), melt the chocolate with the sherry and butter in a bowl over hot water. Gradually add the sugar, beating well until the mixture is glossy. Spread over the top and sides of the cake, using a warmed palette knife. Leave until set.

Decorate the cake with piped cream, cherries and peppermint creams.

Makes one 20 cm/8 inch cake

Chocolate Chestnut Gâteau

METRIC/IMPERIAL
25 g/1 oz cocoa powder
1 tablespoon hot water
175 g/6 oz Muscovado sugar
175 g/6 oz unsalted butter
3 eggs, beaten
175 g/6 oz self-raising flour, sifted
Filling:
175 g/6 oz plain chocolate
50 g/2 oz butter
1 × 225 g/8 oz can sweetened
  chestnut purée
2-3 tablespoons sugar
Topping:
150 ml/¼ pint double cream,
  whipped

AMERICAN
¼ cup unsweetened cocoa
1 tablespoon hot water
1 cup Barbados sugar
¾ cup sweet butter
3 eggs, beaten
1½ cups self-rising flour, sifted
Filling:
1 cup semi-sweet chocolate chips
¼ cup butter
1 cup sweetened chestnut purée
2-3 tablespoons sugar
Topping:
⅔ cup heavy cream, whipped

Blend the cocoa with the hot water and set aside to cool. Cream the sugar and butter together until light and fluffy. Beat in the blended cocoa. Gradually beat in the eggs with a little of the flour. Fold in the remaining flour. Divide the mixture between two lined and greased 20 cm/8 inch sandwich tins (cake layer pans) and bake in a moderately hot oven (190°C/375°F, Gas Mark 5) for 20 to 25 minutes. Turn onto a wire rack to cool.

To make the filling, melt the chocolate with the butter in a bowl over hot water. Beat well and remove from the heat. Gradually beat in the chestnut purée and sugar to taste. Slice both cakes in half and sandwich the four layers together with chestnut chocolate purée, reserving a little for decoration.

Spread the cream over the top of the cake. Using a piping bag, fitted with a small plain nozzle, pipe the reserved chestnut purée around the top of the cake.

Makes one 20 cm/8 inch cake

Chocolate Log

METRIC/IMPERIAL

3 eggs, separated
75 g/3 oz caster sugar
50 g/2 oz plain flour
25 g/1 oz cocoa powder
Chocolate buttercream:
25 g/1 oz cocoa powder
1 tablespoon hot water
100 g/4 oz butter
225 g/8 oz icing sugar, sifted
To finish:
icing sugar for dusting

AMERICAN

3 eggs, separated
6 tablespoons sugar
½ cup all-purpose flour
¼ cup unsweetened cocoa
Chocolate buttercream:
¼ cup unsweetened cocoa
1 tablespoon hot water
½ cup butter
1 ¾ cups confectioners' sugar, sifted
To finish:
confectioners' sugar for dusting

Whisk the egg yolks and sugar together until thick and creamy. Sift the flour with the cocoa and fold into the mixture. Whisk the egg whites until stiff and fold in. Turn into a lined and greased 30 × 20 cm/12 × 8 inch Swiss roll tin (jelly roll pan) and spread evenly. Cook in a hot oven (220°C/425°F, Gas Mark 7) for 8 to 10 minutes until springy to the touch.

Turn onto a piece of sugared greaseproof (waxed) paper, remove the lining paper and trim the edges of the sponge. Roll up with the paper inside and leave until cold.

To prepare the buttercream, mix the cocoa and water together. Beat the butter and sugar together until soft, then add the cocoa mixture and beat until smooth.

Unroll the sponge, remove the paper, and spread with half the buttercream. Re-roll carefully and cover with the remaining buttercream. Mark with a fork to resemble the bark of a log, dust with icing (confectioners') sugar and top with a holly sprig.

Makes one 20 cm/8 inch chocolate log

CHOCOLATE LOG
(Photograph: British Egg Information Service)

Black Forest Gâteau with Ice Cream

METRIC/IMPERIAL	AMERICAN
6 eggs	*6 eggs*
175 g/6 oz caster sugar	*¾ cup sugar*
175 g/6 oz plain flour	*1½ cups all-purpose flour*
25 g/1 oz cocoa powder	*¼ cup unsweetened cocoa*
1 × 450 g/1 lb jar Morello black cherries	*1 × 1 lb can Morello bing cherries*
3 tablespoons rum	*3 tablespoons rum*
500 ml/18 fl oz vanilla ice cream	*2¼ cups vanilla ice cream*
grated plain chocolate to decorate	*grated semi-sweet chocolate to decorate*

Place the eggs and sugar in a bowl over a pan of hot water. Whisk until the mixture is thick and pale in colour. Remove from the heat and whisk until cool. Sift together the flour and cocoa and fold into the mixture.

Divide the mixture between three greased and lined 23 cm/9 inch sandwich tins (cake layer pans). Bake in a moderately hot oven (190°C/375°F, Gas Mark 5) for 15 minutes. Turn out onto a wire rack to cool.

Drain the cherries, reserving 4 tablespoons of the juice; mix this with the rum. Place one sponge layer on a serving dish and sprinkle with a third of the juice. Cover with one third of the ice cream and arrange half of the cherries on top. Repeat these layers once, then cover with the top sponge layer. Sprinkle with the remaining juice and top with the rest of the ice cream. Decorate with grated chocolate. Serve immediately.

Serves 8

Chilled Chocolate Roll Gâteau

METRIC/IMPERIAL

2 tablespoons cocoa powder
1 tablespoon hot water
100 g/4 oz unsalted butter
100 g/4 oz caster sugar
1 egg
2 tablespoons Crême de Menthe
 liqueur (optional)
175 g/6 oz digestive biscuits,
 crushed
50 g/2 oz blanched almonds, toasted
 and chopped
To decorate:
300 ml/½ pint double cream,
 whipped
50 g/2 oz plain chocolate, grated

AMERICAN

2 tablespoons unsweetened cocoa
1 tablespoon hot water
½ cup sweet butter
½ cup sugar
1 egg
2 tablespoons Crême de Menthe
 liqueur (optional)
1½ cups crushed Graham Crackers
½ cup blanched almonds, toasted
 and chopped
To decorate:
1¼ cups heavy cream, whipped
2 squares semi-sweet chocolate,
 grated

Blend the cocoa with the water and leave to cool. Cream the butter and sugar together until light and fluffy. Beat in the egg and liqueur, if using. Stir in the blended cocoa, then add the remaining ingredients and mix to a stiff paste. Shape into a roll, about 6 cm/2½ inches in diameter and place on a serving plate. Cover and chill for 1 to 2 hours until firm.

Spread half the cream over the roll, to cover it completely. Put the remaining cream into a piping bag fitted with a fluted nozzle and pipe along the centre of the roll. Sprinkle with grated chocolate and serve chilled.

Makes one chocolate roll

Mocha Slice

METRIC/IMPERIAL
3 eggs
75 g/3 oz caster sugar
75 g/3 oz plain flour
2 tablespoons cocoa powder
50 g/2 oz butter, melted
3-4 tablespoons sherry
Coffee buttercream:
100 g/4 oz butter
200 g/7 oz icing sugar, sifted
2 teaspoons instant coffee powder
1 teaspoon hot water
To decorate:
75 g/3 oz walnut halves
4 chocolate flakes, halved
3 glacé cherries
25 g/1 oz plain chocolate, melted

AMERICAN
3 eggs
6 tablespoons sugar
3/4 cup all-purpose flour
2 tablespoons unsweetened cocoa
1/4 cup butter, melted
3-4 tablespoons sherry
Coffee buttercream:
1/2 cup butter
1 1/2 cups confectioners' sugar, sifted
2 teaspoons instant coffee powder
1 teaspoon hot water
To decorate:
3/4 cup halved, shelled walnuts
4 chocolate flakes, halved
3 candied cherries
1 square semi-sweet chocolate, melted

Whisk the eggs and sugar together until thick and pale. Sift the flour and cocoa together and carefully fold into the mixture together with the melted butter.

Spoon into a lined and greased 30 × 20 cm/12 × 8 inch Swiss roll tin (jelly roll pan). Bake in a moderately hot oven (200°C/400°F, Gas Mark 6) for about 20 minutes until golden and springy to the touch. Turn out, remove the paper and cool on a wire rack. Cut the cake into 4 pieces, each 7.5 × 20 cm/3 × 8 inches, and sprinkle with the sherry.

Cream the butter and icing (confectioners') sugar together. Dissolve the coffee powder in the water then beat into the mixture. Sandwich the cake together with half the buttercream. Spread the remainder over the top and sides of the cake.

Set aside 4 walnut halves; chop the rest and press onto the sides of the cake. Decorate the top with the walnut halves, chocolate flakes and cherries. Pipe the melted chocolate in lines over the top.
Makes one 20 cm/8 inch cake

MOCHA SLICE, JAM JEWELS (page 22),
CHOCOLATE SPONGE CREAM (page 54)
(Photograph: Cadbury Typhoo Advisory Service)

Chocolate Peach Crunch

METRIC/IMPERIAL
175 g/6 oz cream cheese
100 g/4 oz plain chocolate
50 g/2 oz blanched almonds,
  chopped
100 g/4 oz semi-sweet biscuits,
  crushed
1 × 439 g/15½ oz can sliced
  peaches, drained

AMERICAN
¾ cup cream cheese
4 squares semi-sweet chocolate
½ cup chopped blanched almonds
1 cup crushed semi-sweet cookies
1 × 15½ oz can sliced peaches,
  drained

Beat the cream cheese until smooth. Melt the chocolate in a bowl over hot water and beat in the cream cheese. Mix in the almonds and biscuit (cookie) crumbs.

Reserve a few peaches for decoration; coarsely chop the remainder. Press half the chocolate mixture into a greased 18 cm/7 inch loose-bottomed cake tin (springform pan). Arrange the peaches on top and cover with the remaining chocolate mixture. Chill until firm.

Turn out and cut into wedges before serving, with cream.
Makes one 18 cm/7 inch cake

Chocolate Whisky Cake

METRIC/IMPERIAL
2 eggs
1 tablespoon caster sugar
225 g/8 oz unsalted butter, melted
225 g/8 oz plain chocolate, melted
2 tablespoons Scotch whisky
225 g/8 oz digestive biscuits,
  broken
50 g/2 oz chopped nuts

AMERICAN
2 eggs
1 tablespoon sugar
½ lb sweet butter, melted
½ lb semi-sweet chocolate, melted
2 tablespoons Scotch whisky
½ lb Graham crackers, broken
½ cup chopped nuts

Beat the eggs and sugar together until thick and creamy. Gradually add the melted butter and then the melted chocolate, beating all the time. Fold in the whisky, biscuits (crackers) and nuts.

Spread into a greased 18 cm/7 inch loose-bottomed flan tin (pie pan) and chill before serving, with whipped cream or ice cream.
Makes one 18 cm/7 inch cake

COLD DESSERTS

Chocolate Soufflé

METRIC/IMPERIAL	AMERICAN
300 ml/½ pint milk	1¼ cups milk
1 tablespoon sherry	1 tablespoon sherry
2 eggs, separated	2 eggs, separated
25 g/1 oz plain flour	¼ cup all-purpose flour
50 g/2 oz sugar	¼ cup sugar
100 g/4 oz plain chocolate, melted	⅔ cup semi-sweet chocolate chips, melted
15 g/½ oz gelatine	2 envelopes gelatin
2 tablespoons water	2 tablespoons water
300 ml/½ pint whipping cream, whipped	1¼ cups whipping cream, whipped
few drops of vanilla essence	few drops of vanilla extract
chocolate decorations (see page 8)	chocolate decorations (see page 8)

Place the milk in a pan with the sherry and bring almost to the boil. Mix the egg yolks with the flour and sugar in a bowl. Blend this with a little of the hot milk and when smooth pour on the remaining milk. Return to the pan and bring to the boil, stirring all the time. Simmer for 2 to 3 minutes then remove from the heat. Stir in the melted chocolate, cover and leave to cool.

Dissolve the gelatine with the water in a cup placed in a pan of hot water. Fold this into the chocolate mixture with half the cream. Stiffly whisk the egg whites and fold into the mixture. Pour into a prepared, lightly greased 15 cm/6 inch soufflé dish and chill until set.

Just before serving, mix the rest of the cream with vanilla essence (extract). Remove the collar and spread a little cream over the top and sides of the soufflé. Decorate with piped cream and chocolate curls.

Serves 4 to 6

Note: To prepare a soufflé dish, tie a strip of folded greaseproof (waxed) paper around the dish to extend about 5 cm/2 inches above the rim.

Chocolate Mousse

METRIC/IMPERIAL
100 g/4 oz plain chocolate
300 ml/½ pint milk
3 eggs, separated
50 g/2 oz caster sugar
¼ teaspoon ground ginger
15 g/½ oz gelatine
2 tablespoons water
250 ml/8 fl oz double cream,
 whipped
To decorate:
whipped cream
chopped nuts

AMERICAN
⅔ cup semi-sweet chocolate chips
1¼ cups milk
3 eggs, separated
¼ cup sugar
¼ teaspoon ground ginger
2 envelopes gelatin
2 tablespoons water
1 cup heavy cream, whipped
To decorate:
whipped cream
chopped nuts

Melt the chocolate with the milk in a pan over a gentle heat. Cream the egg yolks, sugar and ground ginger together. Pour on the chocolate flavoured milk, stir well and return to the pan. Cook the custard gently, without allowing it to boil, stirring continuously. Strain into a bowl and leave to cool.

Dissolve the gelatine with the water in a cup placed in hot water. When dissolved, add to the custard. As the custard thickens fold in the cream. Whisk the egg whites lightly and fold into the mixture. Pour into individual glass dishes and leave to set.

To serve, pipe rosettes of cream on the top of each mousse and sprinkle with chopped nuts.
Serves 4

CHOCOLATE MOUSSE
(Photograph: Cadbury Typhoo Advisory Service)

Chocolate Syllabub

METRIC/IMPERIAL
1 tablespoon cocoa powder
120 ml/4 fl oz hot water
2 tablespoons Orange Curaçao or
  Cointreau
50 g/2 oz sugar
300 ml/½ pint double cream

AMERICAN
1 tablespoon unsweetened cocoa
½ cup hot water
2 tablespoons orange liqueur
  (Curaçao)
¼ cup sugar
1¼ cups heavy cream

Blend the cocoa with the water and leave to cool. Place the cocoa, orange liqueur, sugar and cream in a bowl and whisk until stiff.

Pile into individual glass dishes and chill in a refrigerator. Serve with langue de chat biscuits (cookies).
Serves 6

Caramel Delight

METRIC/IMPERIAL
3 Mars bars or other chocolate
  caramel bars
1 tablespoon coffee powder
2 tablespoons hot water
6 egg whites
grated plain chocolate to decorate

AMERICAN
3 chocolate caramel bars
1 tablespoon coffee powder
2 tablespoons hot water
6 egg whites
grated semi-sweet chocolate to
  decorate

Melt the Mars (caramel) bars in a bowl over hot water. Dissolve the coffee in the hot water, add to the Mars (caramel) bars and beat until smooth. Leave to cool.

Whisk the egg whites until stiff and gradually fold into the caramel mixture. Spoon into individual glass dishes, and sprinkle with chocolate to serve.
Serves 4

Chocolate Cheesecake

METRIC/IMPERIAL
Base:
100 g/4 oz butter
225 g/8 oz digestive biscuits,
 crushed
50 g/2 oz sugar
Topping:
2 tablespoons cocoa powder
300 ml/½ pint hot water
225 g/8 oz cottage cheese
75 g/3 oz sugar
grated rind and juice of 1 orange
50 g/2 oz plain chocolate
15 g/½ oz gelatine
To decorate:
whipped cream
grated plain chocolate

AMERICAN
Base:
½ cup butter
2 cups crushed Graham crackers
¼ cup sugar
Topping:
2 tablespoons unsweetened cocoa
1 ¼ cups hot water
½ lb curd cheese
6 tablespoons sugar
grated rind and juice of 1 orange
⅓ cup semi-sweet chocolate chips
2 envelopes gelatin
To decorate:
whipped cream
grated semi-sweet chocolate

Melt the butter in a pan and add the digestive biscuits (Graham crackers) and sugar. Mix well and press into the base of a 23 cm/9 inch flan dish (pie pan).

To make the topping, blend the cocoa with a little of the hot water. Add the remaining water and leave to cool. Pour into an electric blender with the cheese, sugar and grated orange rind. Blend until smooth.

Melt the chocolate in a bowl over hot water. Remove from the heat and gradually blend into the cheese mixture. Mix the gelatine with the orange juice in a cup and place in a pan of hot water to dissolve. Stir into the chocolate and cheese mixture. Pour over the cooled biscuit (cracker) base and place in the refrigerator to set.

Serve decorated with piped cream and grated chocolate.

Serves 6 to 8

Crunchy Orange Flan

METRIC/IMPERIAL
Base:
25 g/1 oz plain chocolate
40 g/1½ oz butter
50 g/2 oz walnuts, finely chopped
100 g/4 oz digestive biscuits,
  crushed
Topping:
2 tablespoons orange marmalade
300 ml/½ pint double cream
1 tablespoon sugar
1 × 200 g/7 oz can mandarin
  oranges, drained and chopped

AMERICAN
Base:
¼ cup semi-sweet chocolate chips
3 tablespoons butter
½ cup finely chopped walnuts
1 cup crushed Graham crackers
Topping:
2 tablespoons orange marmalade
1¼ cups heavy cream
1 tablespoon sugar
1 × 7 oz can mandarin oranges,
  drained and chopped

Melt the chocolate and butter in a pan over low heat. Mix with the walnuts and biscuits (crackers). Press the mixture into the base of a 20 cm/8 inch loose-bottomed flan tin (pie pan). Chill until firm, then carefully remove from the tin (pan) and transfer to a serving plate.

Spread the marmalade over the flan base. Whip the cream and mix with the sugar and the mandarin oranges. Pile on top of the flan base and chill before serving.
Serves 6

Chocolate Pear Flan

METRIC/IMPERIAL
100 g/4 oz plain chocolate, grated
75 g/3 oz butter
225 g/8 oz wholemeal biscuits,
  crushed
2 × 411 g/14½ oz cans pear halves
2 teaspoons arrowroot

AMERICAN
4 squares semi-sweet chocolate,
  grated
6 tablespoons butter
2 cups crushed Graham crackers
2 × 14½ oz cans pear halves
2 teaspoons arrowroot flour

Melt half the chocolate and the butter in a pan over low heat and mix with the biscuits (crackers). Press the mixture into the base and sides of an 18 cm/7 inch loose-bottomed fluted flan tin (pie pan). Chill until firm, then carefully remove the flan from the tin (pan) and transfer to a serving plate.

Drain the pears (reserving the juice) and arrange on the base of the flan. Blend half the juice with the arrowroot, place in a pan and bring to the boil, stirring, until the mixture thickens and clears. Pour over the pears and leave to set.

Sprinkle with the remaining chocolate and serve with cream.
Serves 6

CHOCOLATE PEAR FLAN
(Photograph: Canned Food Advisory Service)

Ice Cream with Chocolate Sauce

METRIC/IMPERIAL	AMERICAN
500 ml/18 fl oz vanilla ice cream	2¼ cups vanilla ice cream
Chocolate Sauce:	**Chocolate Sauce:**
175 g/6 oz plain chocolate, chopped	1 cup semi-sweet chocolate chips
150 ml/¼ pint water	⅔ cup water
1 teaspoon instant coffee powder (optional)	1 teaspoon instant coffee powder (optional)
100 g/4 oz sugar	½ cup sugar

To make the sauce, melt the chocolate, 2 tablespoons of the water and the coffee, if using, in a pan over a gentle heat. Stir until smooth and add the remaining water and sugar. Simmer uncovered for 10 minutes and serve hot or cold with the ice cream.
Serves 4

Note: As an alternative, melt 3 Mars Bars (chocolate caramel bars) with 4 tablespoons milk in a bowl over hot water. Stir until smooth.

Chocolate Apricot Bombe

METRIC/IMPERIAL	AMERICAN
50 g/2 oz plain chocolate	⅓ cup semi-sweet chocolate chips
300 ml/½ pint double cream, whipped, or 2 packets Bird's Dream Topping made up with 300 ml/½ pint milk	1¼ cups heavy cream, whipped, or 2 packets Dream Whip made up with 1¼ cups milk
1 × 425 g/15 oz can apricots, drained	1 × 15 oz can apricots, drained
2 teaspoons brandy	2 teaspoons brandy
juice of ½ orange	juice of ½ orange
1 tablespoon sugar	1 tablespoon sugar
apricot halves to decorate	apricot halves to decorate

Melt the chocolate in a bowl over hot water and stir in half of the cream or Dream Topping (Whip). Use to line a 900 ml/1½ pint freezerproof mould. Cover and freeze until firm.

Purée the apricots using an electric blender or sieve. Add the brandy and orange juice. Mix the apricot mixture with the rest of the cream or Dream Topping (Whip) and the sugar and stir well. Turn into the centre of the frozen bombe. Cover and freeze until firm.

Transfer to the refrigerator for about 1 hour before serving. Unmould and decorate with apricots if liked.
Serves 6

Chocolate Orange Ice Cream

METRIC/IMPERIAL
1 teaspoon gelatine
2 tablespoons water
450 ml/3/4 pint milk
1 tablespoon custard powder
3 tablespoons caster sugar
100 g/4 oz unsalted butter
4 tablespoons frozen concentrated
  orange juice
100 g/4 oz plain chocolate, roughly
  chopped

AMERICAN
1 teaspoon gelatin
2 tablespoons water
2 cups milk
1 tablespoon Bird's English
  Imported Dessert Mix
3 tablespoons sugar
1/2 cup sweet butter
4 tablespoons frozen concentrated
  orange juice
2/3 cup semi-sweet chocolate chips

Dissolve the gelatine and the water in a cup placed in a pan of hot water. Make up the custard with the milk, custard powder (Dessert Mix) and sugar. Pour into an electric blender, add the gelatine, butter and orange juice and blend until smooth.

Pour into a rigid freezerproof container and leave until cool. Cover, seal and freeze for about 1 hour, until almost frozen. Remove from the freezer and stir in the chocolate. Beat well, then refreeze until firm. Serve with wafer biscuits.
Serves 6

Chocolate Mint Ice Cream

METRIC/IMPERIAL
50 g/2 oz plain chocolate
300 ml/1/2 pint double cream,
  whipped, or 2 packets Dream
  Topping made up with
  300 ml/1/2 pint milk
few drops of peppermint oil or
  essence

AMERICAN
1/3 cup semi-sweet chocolate chips
1 1/4 cups heavy cream, whipped, or
  2 packets Dream Whip made up
  with 1 1/4 cups milk
few drops of peppermint oil or
  extract

Melt the chocolate over hot water. Mix half the cream or Dream Topping (Whip) with the chocolate. Put half of the chocolate mixture into a 450 g/1 lb loaf tin (pan) and place in the freezer until just firm.

Flavour the remaining cream or Dream Topping (Whip) with peppermint. Spread carefully over the layer of chocolate ice cream. Freeze until just firm. Top with the remaining chocolate mixture and freeze thoroughly. Transfer to the refrigerator 20 minutes before serving.
Serves 6

Citrus Crunch

METRIC/IMPERIAL
225 g/8 oz fresh breadcrumbs
75 g/3 oz butter
40 g/1½ oz demerara sugar
50 g/2 oz plain chocolate, grated
1 × 312 g/11 oz can mandarin
  oranges, drained
300 ml/½ pint double cream
grated rind and juice of ½ lemon
grated plain chocolate to decorate

AMERICAN
4 cups fresh bread crumbs
6 tablespoons butter
⅓ cup raw sugar
2 squares semi-sweet chocolate,
  grated
1 × 11 oz can mandarin oranges,
  drained
1¼ cups heavy cream
grated rind and juice of ½ lemon
grated semi-sweet chocolate to
  decorate

Fry the breadcrumbs in the butter until crisp. Leave to cool. Stir in the sugar and chocolate. Reserve a few mandarins for decoration and purée the remainder in an electric blender or sieve. Add the cream, lemon rind and juice and whisk until thick.

Place alternate layers of breadcrumbs and orange cream in tall individual glasses. Decorate with the mandarins and chocolate. Chill before serving.
Serves 4

Chocolate Chestnut Dessert

METRIC/IMPERIAL
100 g/4 oz unsalted butter
100 g/4 oz caster sugar
225 g/8 oz plain chocolate, melted
1 × 440 g/15½ oz can
  unsweetened chestnut purée
few drops of vanilla essence
To decorate:
150 ml/¼ pint double cream,
  whipped
1 × 200 g/7 oz can mandarin
  oranges, drained

AMERICAN
½ cup sweet butter
½ cup sugar
½ lb semi-sweet chocolate, melted
1 × 15½ oz can unsweetened
  chestnut purée
few drops of vanilla extract
To decorate:
⅔ cup heavy cream, whipped
1 × 7 oz can mandarin oranges,
  drained

Cream together the butter and sugar. Add the chocolate, chestnut purée and vanilla essence (extract). Beat together until smooth and creamy.

Turn the mixture into a lightly greased and base-lined 450 g/1 lb loaf tin (pan). Place in the refrigerator overnight. To serve, turn out and decorate with piped cream and mandarin oranges.
Serves 8

CITRUS CRUNCH
(Photograph: Flour Advisory Bureau)

Chocolate Sponge Cream

METRIC/IMPERIAL
1 whisked sponge (see recipe)
24 sponge fingers (approximately)
175 g/6 oz plain chocolate
4 eggs, separated
1 tablespoon instant coffee powder
15 g/½ oz gelatine
4 tablespoons water
300 ml/½ pint double cream,
  lightly whipped
grated plain chocolate to decorate

AMERICAN
1 whisked sponge (see recipe)
24 ladyfingers (approximately)
1 cup semi-sweet chocolate chips
4 eggs, separated
1 tablespoon instant coffee powder
2 envelopes gelatin
4 tablespoons water
1¼ cups heavy cream, lightly
  whipped
grated semi-sweet chocolate to
  decorate

Prepare the whisked sponge mixture as for Chocolate Log (see page 36). Turn into a lined and greased 18 cm/7 inch sandwich tin (layer cake pan) and bake in a moderately hot oven (190°C/375°F, Gas Mark 5) for 20 to 30 minutes. Turn out and cool on a wire rack. Place the cake in the centre of a lightly greased 20 cm/8 inch round loose-bottomed cake tin (springform pan). Trim one rounded end off each finger and arrange upright around the cake.

Melt the chocolate in a bowl over hot water, then beat in the egg yolks and coffee. Dissolve the gelatine with the water in a bowl over hot water. Stir into the chocolate mixture and leave to cool slightly. Whisk the egg whites until stiff. Fold into the chocolate mixture, with a third of the whipped cream. Pour on top of the cake in the tin (pan). Leave in a cool place for several hours to set.

Just before serving, remove the cake from the tin and slide onto a serving plate. To keep the fingers in place tie a ribbon round the pudding. Spread the remaining cream on top and sprinkle with the chocolate.

Makes one 20 cm/8 inch cake

Chocolate and Apricot Rice Cake

METRIC/IMPERIAL
450 ml/¾ pint milk
75 g/3 oz sugar
175 g/6 oz plain chocolate, grated
100 g/4 oz pudding rice
few drops of vanilla essence
15 g/½ oz gelatine
2 tablespoons water
50 g/2 oz butter
12 fresh and ripe or canned apricots
300 ml/½ pint double cream,
  whipped

AMERICAN
2 cups milk
6 tablespoons sugar
1 cup semi-sweet chocolate chips,
  grated
⅔ cup pudding rice (Carolina)
few drops of vanilla extract
2 envelopes gelatin
2 tablespoons water
¼ cup butter
12 fresh and ripe or canned apricots
1¼ cups heavy cream, whipped

Place the milk in a pan with the sugar and chocolate and stir until the chocolate melts. Bring to the boil and then simmer. Drop the rice into boiling water for 2 minutes then drain and add to the milk and chocolate mixture. Stir well and simmer gently for 25 minutes. Add vanilla essence (extract) to taste.

Dissolve the gelatine with the water in a cup placed in a pan of hot water. Stir this into the hot rice mixture with the butter, and leave to cool.

Blanch fresh apricots in boiling water; drain canned apricots. Reserve 4 for the base and dice the rest. Add to the rice mixture with the cream.

Halve the reserved apricots and arrange in the base of a greased 20 cm/8 inch round loose-bottomed cake tin (springform pan). Spread the chocolate rice mixture over the top and place in the refrigerator to set. Turn out and serve with fresh cream.
Serves 6

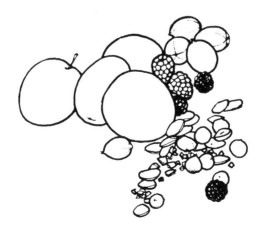

Profiteroles

METRIC/IMPERIAL
50 g/2 oz butter
150 ml/¼ pint water
65 g/2½ oz plain flour, sifted
pinch of salt
2 eggs, beaten
Chocolate Sauce (see page 50)
Filling:
300 ml/½ pint double cream,
 whipped

AMERICAN
¼ cup butter
⅔ cup water
10 tablespoons all-purpose flour,
 sifted
pinch of salt
2 eggs, beaten
Chocolate Sauce (see page 50)
Filling:
1¼ cups heavy cream, whipped

Melt the butter in a pan, add the water and bring to the boil. Remove from the heat, add the flour and salt and beat until the mixture leaves the side of the pan. Add the eggs gradually, beating until the mixture is smooth and glossy.

Place the mixture in a piping bag fitted with a 1 cm/½ inch plain nozzle. Pipe 18 small rounds, well spaced, onto a greased baking sheet. Bake in a hot oven (220°C/425°F, Gas Mark 7) for 15 to 20 minutes.

Remove from the oven and slit the buns along one side. Leave to cool. Fill with the whipped cream and arrange in a pyramid shape on a cake stand. Spoon the hot chocolate sauce over the top before serving.
Serves 6

Chocolate Apples and Pears

METRIC/IMPERIAL
4 firm apples or pears, with stalks
300 ml/½ pint cider
25 g/1 oz sugar
175 g/6 oz plain chocolate

AMERICAN
4 firm apples or pears, with stalks
1¼ cups hard cider
2 tablespoons sugar
1 cup semi-sweet chocolate chips

Leaving the stalk intact, peel the fruit thinly. Carefully core from the bottom, leaving the fruit whole.

Put the cider and sugar in a saucepan and heat gently. Add the fruit and poach gently for about 3 minutes. Remove the fruit before it becomes too soft. Leave to dry and cool on kitchen paper.

Melt the chocolate in a bowl over hot water. Coat the fruit with chocolate, either by dipping it in the chocolate or spooning the chocolate over the fruit. Place in individual dishes or arrange on a large dish. Serve with cream or the reserved cider syrup.
Serves 4

HOT PUDDINGS

Chocolate Fondue

METRIC/IMPERIAL
2 eggs
4 tablespoons sweet white wine
175 g/6 oz plain chocolate, grated

AMERICAN
2 eggs
4 tablespoons sweet white wine
6 squares semi-sweet chocolate, grated

Whisk the eggs and wine together in a bowl until thick. Add the chocolate and place over hot water. Stir until the chocolate has melted and the mixture thickens.

To serve, keep the chocolate mixture warm and have an assortment of fresh fruit, peppermint creams or any other sweets to dip into the fondue.
Serves 8

Chocolate Soufflé

METRIC/IMPERIAL
50 g/2 oz plain chocolate
300 ml/½ pint milk
75 g/3 oz butter
50 g/2 oz plain flour, sifted
3 eggs, separated

AMERICAN
⅓ cup semi-sweet chocolate chips
1¼ cups milk
6 tablespoons butter
½ cup all-purpose flour, sifted
3 eggs, separated

Melt the chocolate with the milk in a pan over gentle heat, stirring occasionally. Melt the butter in another pan and stir in the flour. Gradually add the chocolate milk, stirring all the time. Bring to the boil, then simmer for 3 minutes until thick and smooth. Cover and leave to cool.

Beat the egg yolks into the sauce. Stiffly whisk the whites and gently fold into the chocolate mixture. Spoon into a greased and prepared 1.2 litre/2 pint soufflé dish (see page 43) and cook in a moderately hot oven (190°C/375°F, Gas Mark 5) for 30 to 40 minutes. Serve at once, with cream.
Serves 4

Pancake (Crêpe) Layer Pudding

METRIC/IMPERIAL
Crêpes:
100 g/4 oz plain flour
pinch of salt
1 egg
300 ml/½ pint milk
Filling:
750 g/1½ lb pears, peeled and
  sliced
150 ml/¼ pint water
2 tablespoons sugar
100 g/4 oz plain chocolate
2 tablespoons lemon juice
50 g/2 oz hazelnuts, chopped

AMERICAN
Crêpes:
1 cup all-purpose flour
salt
1 egg
1¼ cups milk
Filling:
1½ lb pears, peeled and sliced
⅔ cup water
2 tablespoons sugar
⅔ cup semi-sweet chocolate chips
2 tablespoons lemon juice
½ cup chopped filberts

To make the crêpes, sift the flour and salt into a bowl, making a well in the centre. Beat the egg with a little of the milk and pour into the well. Beat well, adding the milk gradually to make a smooth batter. Cook as for Banana Cream Pancakes (Crêpes) (see page 60) and keep warm.

Place the pears, water and sugar in a pan and simmer until the pears are tender. Drain and keep warm. Melt the chocolate with the lemon juice in a basin over hot water. Stir in the hazelnuts (filberts) and keep warm.

Place a crêpe on a warmed serving dish, cover with pears and pour over the chocolate mixture. Repeat the layers, finishing with a crêpe. Arrange a few pears in a star design on top. Serve hot with cream.
Serves 4 to 6

Banana Cream Pancakes (Crêpes)

METRIC/IMPERIAL

Pancakes:
100 g/4 oz plain flour, sifted
2 eggs
300 ml/½ pint milk
1 teaspoon lemon juice
1 tablespoon oil
lard

Filling:
6 bananas
2 tablespoons lemon juice
300 ml/½ pint double cream,
  whipped
50 g/2 oz walnuts, chopped

Topping:
½ banana, sliced
Chocolate dessert topping or
Chocolate Sauce (see page 50)

AMERICAN

Crêpes:
1 cup all-purpose flour, sifted
2 eggs
1 ¼ cups milk
1 teaspoon lemon juice
1 tablespoon oil
shortening

Filling:
6 bananas
2 tablespoons lemon juice
1 ¼ cups heavy cream, whipped
½ cup chopped walnuts

Topping:
½ banana, sliced
Chocolate dessert topping or
Chocolate Sauce (see page 50)

To make the pancakes (crêpes), put the flour into a bowl and make a well in the centre. Add the eggs, beat well, adding the milk gradually to make a smooth batter. Finally, stir in the lemon juice and oil.

Grease a heavy based frying pan (skillet) with a little lard (shortening) and place over moderate heat. When hot, pour in sufficient batter to cover the base of the pan. Cook until golden on the underside, then turn over and cook on the other side. Repeat with the remaining batter. Stack the pancakes (crêpes) between sheets of greaseproof (wax) paper and keep warm.

To make the filling, slice the bananas and toss in the lemon juice; add the cream and nuts. Divide the mixture between the pancakes (crêpes) and roll up. Serve topped with banana slices and chocolate sauce.

Serves 4 to 6

Alternative Chocolate Filling:
Melt 75 g/3 oz plain chocolate (½ cup semi-sweet chocolate chips) in a bowl over hot water. When smooth, gradually beat in 350 g/12 oz cottage cheese (¾ lb curd cheese) until thoroughly mixed. (For a smoother texture sieve the cheese before adding to the chocolate.) Add 2 to 3 tablespoons sugar to taste and 3 tablespoons raisins. Fill the pancakes (crêpes) and serve with chocolate sauce.

BANANA CREAM PANCAKES (CRÊPES)
(Photograph: Jif Dessert Toppings)

Mandarin Chocolate Crunch

METRIC/IMPERIAL
1 × 300 g/11 oz can mandarin
  oranges, drained
300 ml/½ pint milk
  (approximately)
3 tablespoons custard powder
1 tablespoon caster sugar
Topping:
4 slices white bread
2 tablespoons cocoa powder
50 g/2 oz butter
50 g/2 oz soft brown sugar

AMERICAN
1 × 11 oz can mandarin oranges
1¼ cups milk (approximately)
3 tablespoons Bird's English
  Imported Dessert Mix
1 tablespoon sugar
Topping:
4 slices white bread
2 tablespoons unsweetened cocoa
¼ cup butter
⅓ cup light brown sugar

Drain the mandarins, reserving the juice; make up to 450 ml/¾ pint (2 cups) with milk.

Blend the custard powder (Dessert Mix) and sugar with a little of the orange and milk mixture. Gradually add the remaining liquid and then pour into a pan. Bring to the boil, stirring all the time. Reserve a few of the mandarin oranges and add the rest to the custard. Pour the mixture into a heatproof dish, cover and keep warm.

Remove the crusts from the bread and cut into 1 cm/½ inch cubes. Put the cocoa, butter and sugar in a pan and heat gently, stirring until melted. Add the bread and stir until well coated with the chocolate mixture.

Pile on top of the custard mixture and place under the grill (broiler) for a few minutes until the bread is crisp. Decorate with the reserved mandarin oranges and serve at once.
Serves 4

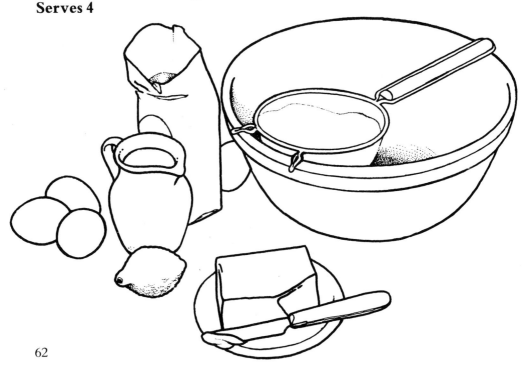

Chocolate Peach Crumble

METRIC/IMPERIAL
175 g/6 oz plain flour, sifted
75 g/3 oz butter
75 g/3 oz soft brown sugar
1 × 425 g/15 oz can peach slices,
  drained
100 g/4 oz plain chocolate, grated

AMERICAN
1½ cups all-purpose flour, sifted
6 tablespoons butter
½ cup light brown sugar
1 × 15 oz can peach slices, drained
4 squares semi-sweet chocolate,
  grated

To make the crumble, place the flour in a bowl and rub in the butter until the mixture resembles fine breadcrumbs. Stir in the sugar.

Butter a 900 ml/1½ pint ovenproof dish and fill with layers of crumble mixture, peach slices and grated chocolate, finishing with crumble. Bake in a moderately hot oven (190°C/375°F, Gas Mark 5) for about 35 minutes until golden. Serve hot with cream.
Serves 4 to 6

Chocolate Sponge Cups

METRIC/IMPERIAL
75 g/3 oz self-raising flour
salt
50 g/2 oz shredded suet
50 g/2 oz caster sugar
25 g/1 oz cocoa powder
1 tablespoon hot water
1 egg, beaten
2-3 tablespoons milk

AMERICAN
¾ cup self-rising flour
salt
⅓ cup shredded suet
¼ cup sugar
¼ cup unsweetened cocoa
1 tablespoon hot water
1 egg, beaten
2-3 tablespoons milk

Sift the flour and salt into a bowl and mix in the suet and the sugar. Blend the cocoa with the hot water and beat into the mixture with the egg and sufficient milk to produce a soft dropping consistency.

Divide the mixture between 6 greased dariole moulds. Cover with greased foil or greaseproof (wax) paper and tie securely. Steam for 30 minutes.

Turn out onto individual warmed serving plates. Serve with chocolate sauce (see page 50).
Serves 6

Note: This mixture can also be steamed in a greased 600 ml/1 pint basin (mold) for 1½ hours.

Chocolate Upside Down Pudding

METRIC/IMPERIAL
Topping:
50 g/2 oz unsalted butter
50 g/2 oz caster sugar
7 pineapple rings
7 glacé cherries
Sponge:
150 g/5 oz self-raising flour
25 g/1 oz cocoa powder
100 g/4 oz unsalted butter
100 g/4 oz caster sugar
2 eggs
2 tablespoons milk
Sauce:
50 g/2 oz unsalted butter
100 g/4 oz plain chocolate
50 g/2 oz caster sugar
120 ml/4 fl oz milk

AMERICAN
Topping:
¼ cup sweet butter
¼ cup sugar
7 pineapple rings
7 candied cherries
Sponge:
1¼ cups self-rising flour
¼ cup unsweetened cocoa
½ cup sweet butter
½ cup sugar
2 eggs
2 tablespoons milk
Sauce:
¼ cup sweet butter
⅔ cup semi-sweet chocolate chips
¼ cup sugar
½ cup milk

To make the topping, cream the butter and sugar together and spread over the base of a 20 cm/8 inch cake tin (pan). Arrange the pineapple rings and cherries on top.

Sift the flour and cocoa together. Cream the butter and sugar together, then beat in the eggs with the milk and a little flour. Fold in the remaining flour mixture. Spoon the mixture over the fruit and bake in a moderate oven (180°C/350°F, Gas Mark 4) for 40 to 50 minutes until well risen.

Meanwhile make the sauce: melt the butter and chocolate together in a bowl over hot water. Place the sugar and milk in a pan and heat gently, stirring until the sugar has dissolved. Increase the heat and bring almost to boiling point. Add to the chocolate mixture and simmer until the sauce is thick.

To serve, turn the cake out onto a warmed serving dish and hand the hot sauce separately.
Serves 6 to 8

CHOCOLATE UPSIDE DOWN PUDDING
(Dutch Dairy Bureau)

Chocolate Chip Pudding

METRIC/IMPERIAL
175 g/6 oz self-raising flour, sifted
½ teaspoon baking powder
75 g/3 oz fresh white breadcrumbs
100 g/4 oz shredded suet
100 g/4 oz caster sugar
100 g/4 oz plain chocolate drops
2 eggs, beaten
150 ml/¼ pint milk

AMERICAN
1½ cups self-rising flour
½ teaspoon baking powder
1½ cups fresh white bread crumbs
⅔ cup shredded suet
½ cup sugar
⅔ cup semi-sweet chocolate chips
2 eggs, beaten
⅔ cup milk

Sift the flour and baking powder into a bowl. Add the breadcrumbs, suet, sugar and chocolate and mix together. Add the beaten eggs and milk and mix to a soft consistency. Spoon into a greased 1.2 litre/2 pint pudding basin (mold) and cover with greased foil or greaseproof (parchment) paper and tie securely. Steam for 1¼ to 1½ hours.

Turn out onto a serving dish and serve with chocolate sauce (see page 50).
Serves 4 to 6

Chocolate Cherry Pudding

METRIC/IMPÈRIAL
100 g/4 oz butter
100 g/4 oz caster sugar
2 eggs
100 g/4 oz self-raising flour, sifted
40 g/1½ oz glacé cherries, quartered
40 g/1½ oz plain chocolate, grated

AMERICAN
½ cup butter
¼ cup sugar
2 eggs
1 cup self-rising flour, sifted
¼ cup candied cherries, quartered
1½ squares semi-sweet chocolate, grated

Cream the butter and sugar together until light and fluffy. Beat in the eggs with a little flour, then fold in the rest of the flour. Stir in the cherries and grated chocolate.

Spoon the mixture into a greased 900 ml/1½ pint pudding basin (mold). Cover with greased foil or greaseproof (wax) paper and tie securely. Steam for 1 to 1½ hours.

Turn out onto a serving dish and serve with hot chocolate sauce (see page 50).
Serves 4 to 6

Chocolate Pudding with Orange Sauce

METRIC/IMPERIAL
175 g/6 oz margarine
175 g/6 oz caster sugar
3 eggs, beaten
175 g/6 oz self-raising flour, sifted
50 g/2 oz plain chocolate, finely chopped
25 g/1 oz cocoa powder
1 tablespoon hot water
Sauce:
2 oranges
300 ml/½ pint water
15 g/½ oz margarine
15 g/½ oz plain flour
1-2 tablespoons sugar

AMERICAN
¾ cup margarine
¾ cup sugar
3 eggs, beaten
1 ½ cups self-rising flour, sifted
⅓ cup semi-sweet chocolate chips
¼ cup unsweetened cocoa
1 tablespoon hot water
Sauce:
2 oranges
1 ¼ cups water
1 tablespoon margarine
2 tablespoons all-purpose flour
1-2 tablespoons sugar

Beat the margarine and sugar together until light and fluffy. Gradually beat in the eggs with some of the flour. Fold in the remaining flour with the chocolate pieces. Blend the cocoa with the hot water and stir into the mixture.

Spoon the mixture into a greased 1.5 litre/2½ pint pudding basin (mold). Cover with foil, or greased greaseproof (wax) paper and tie securely. Steam for about 1½ hours.

To make the sauce, thinly peel the rind from the oranges and shred finely. Place in a saucepan with the water and bring to the boil, then simmer for 20 minutes. Add the juice of both oranges and leave to one side. Melt the margarine in a saucepan, stir in the flour and cook for 1 to 2 minutes. Gradually stir in the orange liquid, then bring to the boil, stirring all the time. Simmer for a few minutes and then sweeten to taste with sugar.

Turn the chocolate pudding out onto a serving dish and serve with the hot sauce.
Serves 6 to 8

CONFECTIONERY

Kirsch Truffles

METRIC/IMPERIAL
120 ml/4 fl oz whipping cream
350 g/12 oz plain chocolate, grated
25 g/1 oz unsalted butter
1-2 tablespoons Kirsch

AMERICAN
½ cup whipping cream
¾ lb semi-sweet chocolate, grated
2 tablespoons sweet butter
1-2 tablespoons Kirsch

Heat the cream in a saucepan to just below boiling point. Remove from the heat and add half the chocolate and the butter. Whisk until smooth and thickened. Cool to room temperature, add the Kirsch and beat thoroughly. Chill until firm, then shape the mixture into small balls, about 2.5 cm/1 inch in diameter.

Melt the remaining chocolate in a bowl over hot water. Skewer each truffle on a cocktail stick (toothpick) and dip into the melted chocolate. Stick into a firm base, such as a potato, and leave to set. Remove from the sticks and serve.
Makes 30

WALNUT TRUFFLES *(page 70)*, ALMOND CRUNCH *(page 72)*,
CHOCOLATE-TIPPED MACAROONS *(page 70)*,
KIRSCH TRUFFLES, CHOCOLATE FRUIT CUPS *(page 71)*
(Photograph: Flair Tableware from Ravenhead Glass)

Walnut Truffles

METRIC/IMPERIAL	AMERICAN
175 g/6 oz plain chocolate	1 cup semi-sweet chocolate chips
25 g/1 oz unsalted butter	2 tablespoons sweet butter
1 egg yolk	1 egg yolk
grated rind of 1 orange	grated rind of 1 orange
25 g/1 oz walnuts, finely chopped	1/4 cup finely chopped walnuts
1 tablespoon brandy	1 tablespoon brandy
chocolate vermicelli for coating	chocolate sprinkles for coating

Melt the chocolate in a bowl over hot water. Add the butter, egg yolk, orange rind, walnuts and brandy and beat together for 2 to 3 minutes.

Chill the mixture until firm. Shape into small balls about 2.5 cm/ 1 inch in diameter and coat with vermicelli (chocolate sprinkles).
Makes 20

Chocolate-Tipped Macaroons

METRIC/IMPERIAL	AMERICAN
2 egg whites	2 egg whites
100 g/4 oz caster sugar	1/2 cup sugar
75 g/3 oz ground almonds	3/4 cup ground almonds
50 g/2 oz plain chocolate	1/3 cup semi-sweet chocolate chips

Whisk the egg whites until stiff, then whisk in the sugar, a little at a time. Fold in the ground almonds.

Put the mixture into a piping bag fitted with a 1 cm/1/2 inch plain nozzle and pipe the mixture in 5 cm/2 inch lengths onto a lightly oiled baking sheet. Bake in a cool oven (140°C/275°F, Gas Mark 1) for 1 to 1½ hours. Leave for a few minutes, then transfer to a wire rack and leave to cool.

Melt the chocolate in a bowl over hot water and dip the ends of the macaroons into the chocolate to coat. Leave on the wire rack until set.
Makes 32

Chocolate Fruit Cups

METRIC/IMPERIAL
100 g/4 oz plain chocolate
18 paper sweet cases
Filling:
25 g/1 oz butter
25 g/1 oz blanched almonds, finely chopped
25 g/1 oz walnuts, finely chopped
50 g/2 oz stoned dates, finely chopped
50 g/2 oz raisins, finely chopped
4 glacé cherries, finely chopped
100 g/4 oz cream cheese
grated rind of 1 orange
1 tablespoon orange juice
To decorate:
grated chocolate
chopped glacé cherries (optional)

AMERICAN
⅔ cup semi-sweet chocolate chips
18 paper bonbon cups
Filling:
2 tablespoons butter
¼ cup finely chopped blanched almonds
¼ cup finely chopped walnuts
⅔ cup pitted dates, finely chopped
⅓ cup finely chopped raisins
4 candied cherries, finely chopped
½ cup cream cheese
grated rind of 1 orange
1 tablespoon orange juice
To decorate:
grated chocolate
chopped candied cherries (optional)

To make the chocolate cases, melt the chocolate in a bowl over hot water, stirring occasionally. Place a teaspoon of chocolate in a paper case (bonbon cup) and gently tilt so that the chocolate covers the sides of the case. Repeat with the remaining cases. Chill until set.

Carefully peel off the paper cases (bonbon cups), recoating any cracks with more melted chocolate. Chill until required.

To make the filling, melt the butter in a pan and add the nuts and fruit. Remove from the heat and beat in the cream cheese, orange rind and juice. Leave the mixture to cool.

Fill each chocolate case with about 2 teaspoons of the mixture. Decorate with a little grated chocolate and cherry pieces, if using. Chill until required.

Makes 18

Almond Crunch

METRIC/IMPERIAL	AMERICAN
175 g/6 oz split blanched almonds	1 1/2 cups split blanched almonds
1 tablespoon hot water	1 tablespoon hot water
1 tablespoon instant coffee powder	1 tablespoon instant coffee powder
225 g/8 oz caster sugar	1 cup sugar
175 g/6 oz unsalted butter	3/4 cup sweet butter
100 g/4 oz plain chocolate	2/3 cup semi-sweet chocolate chips

Spread the almonds on a baking sheet and toast under a medium grill (broiler). Leave to cool.

Place the water, coffee, sugar and butter in a saucepan and heat gently, stirring constantly, until the sugar has dissolved. Bring the mixture to the boil and boil until a little of the mixture dropped into a cup of cold water will form a hard ball.

Remove from the heat and stir in three quarters of the toasted almonds. Pour into a greased shallow 20 cm/8 inch square tin (pan) spreading evenly. Chill until set.

Melt the chocolate in a bowl over hot water. Pour the melted chocolate over the toffee and sprinkle with the remaining almonds. Leave until set, then break into pieces.

Makes about 20 pieces

Rum Truffles

METRIC/IMPERIAL	AMERICAN
100 g/4 oz plain chocolate	2/3 cup semi-sweet chocolate chips
50 g/2 oz butter	1/4 cup butter
2 tablespoons rum	2 tablespoons rum
2 egg yolks	2 egg yolks
50 g/2 oz cake crumbs	1 cup cake crumbs
225 g/8 oz icing sugar, sifted	1 3/4 cups sifted confectioners' sugar
drinking chocolate to decorate	sweetened cocoa to decorate

Melt the chocolate and butter in a bowl over hot water, stirring occasionally. Add the rum and egg yolks and mix well. Work in the cake crumbs and icing (confectioners') sugar. Chill until firm.

Shape the mixture into small balls, about 2.5 cm/1 inch in diameter, and roll in drinking chocolate powder (sweetened cocoa).

Makes 35

RUM TRUFFLES, CHOCOLATE RAISIN FUDGE *(page 74),*
ORANGE TRUFFLE CUPS *(page 74)*
(Photograph: Tate and Lyle)

Orange Truffle Cups

METRIC/IMPERIAL
100 g/4 oz plain chocolate
18 paper sweet cases
Filling:
150 g/5 oz plain chocolate
50 g/2 oz unsalted butter
1 egg yolk
grated rind of 1 orange
4 tablespoons Cointreau or orange
 juice
100 g/4 oz wheatmeal biscuits,
 crushed
To decorate:
walnut halves

AMERICAN
2/3 cup semi-sweet chocolate chips
18 paper bonbon cups
Filling:
3/4 cup semi-sweet chocolate chips
1/4 cup sweet butter
1 egg yolk
grated rind of 1 orange
4 tablespoons Cointreau or orange
 juice
1 cup crushed Graham crackers
To decorate:
walnut halves

Make the chocolate cases as for Chocolate Fruit Cups (see page 71) and chill until required.

To make the filling, melt the chocolate in a bowl over hot water. Add the butter, egg yolk, orange rind and liqueur or orange juice. Mix well, then stir in the biscuits (crackers). Leave to cool.

Fill each chocolate case with about 2 teaspoons of the mixture and decorate with walnut halves. Chill until required.
Makes 18

Chocolate Raisin Fudge

METRIC/IMPERIAL
25 g/1 oz butter
4 tablespoons cocoa powder
250 ml/8 fl oz milk
225 g/8 oz soft brown sugar
2 tablespoons raisins
few drops of vanilla essence

AMERICAN
2 tablespoons butter
4 tablespoons unsweetened cocoa
1 cup milk
1 1/3 cups light brown sugar
2 tablespoons raisins
few drops of vanilla extract

Melt the butter in a saucepan. Blend the cocoa with a little of the milk to form a smooth paste, then add the rest of the milk. Add to the butter with the sugar and bring to the boil, stirring.

Continue to boil until a little of the mixture forms a soft ball when dropped into a cup of cold water. Remove from the heat and add the raisins and vanilla essence (extract) to taste. Beat the mixture until smooth and thickened. Pour into a buttered 15 cm/6 inch square tin (pan) and mark into 2.5 cm/1 inch squares. Leave to cool before cutting into pieces.
Makes 36 squares

Crunchy Chocolate Fudge

METRIC/IMPERIAL
175 g/6 oz fine biscuit or cake
  crumbs
2 tablespoons golden syrup
100 g/4 oz unsalted butter
50 g/2 oz sugar
50 g/2 oz cocoa powder
few drops of vanilla essence

AMERICAN
3 cups fine cookie or cake crumbs
2 tablespoons corn syrup
1/2 cup sweet butter
1/4 cup sugar
1/2 cup unsweetened cocoa
few drops of vanilla extract

Spread the crumbs on a baking sheet and bake in a moderate oven (160°C/325°F, Gas Mark 3) for 3 to 5 minutes to crisp.

Place the syrup, butter and sugar in a saucepan and heat until the butter is melted. Stir in the cocoa and cook gently for 2 minutes, stirring constantly. Remove from the heat and stir in the crumbs and vanilla essence (extract) to taste. Mix thoroughly.

Press the mixture into a greased 18 cm/7 inch square tin (pan) and mark into 2.5 cm/1 inch squares. Chill in the refrigerator for 24 hours before cutting.

Makes 49 squares

Caramels

METRIC/IMPERIAL
50 g/2 oz plain chocolate, grated
100 g/4 oz soft brown sugar
150 ml/1/4 pint milk
350 g/12 oz golden syrup
40 g/1 1/2 oz butter
1/4 teaspoon vanilla essence

AMERICAN
1/3 cup semi-sweet chocolate chips
2/3 cup light brown sugar
2/3 cup milk
1 cup light corn syrup
3 tablespoons butter
1/4 teaspoon vanilla extract

Place all the ingredients except the vanilla essence (extract) in a saucepan and bring slowly to the boil, stirring. Continue to boil gently until a little of the mixture forms a hard ball when dropped into a cup of cold water. Remove from the heat and stir in the vanilla essence (extract). Pour into a shallow, well oiled 18 cm/7 inch square tin (pan). Mark into 2.5 cm/1 inch squares and leave to set. When cold, cut into squares.

Makes 49 squares

INDEX

The publishers wish to acknowledge the following photographers:
Bryce Attwell: 29; Robert Golden: 21; Paul Williams: 4, 17, 57, 69, 73
and cover photograph.